Dinosaurs

This book belongs to

_____

Written by Tapasi De
Illustrated by Suman S. Roy

Dinosaurs were reptiles who lived millions of years ago on Earth.

The word 'dinosaur' means
'terrible lizard'.

The first dinosaurs were small and lightly built. They were very active and fast.

Dinosaurs were mostly herbivores. Some dinosaurs were carnivores also like the famous T. Rex.

Some dinosaurs were seed-eaters, fish-eaters, insectivores and also omnivores who ate both plant and meat.

Dinosaurs hatched from eggs.

Dinosaurs usually walked on their toes. Most of them walked on two legs. Some walked on four legs too.

Carnivorous dinosaurs could run quickly. They had large, strong jaws, sharp teeth and deadly claws to kill their prey.

A person who studies dinosaurs is known as a paleontologist.

Some dinosaurs swallowed rocks in order to grind up the food they had eaten.

Carnivorous dinosaurs had a very good eyesight and a keen sense of smell.

The nests of dinosaurs could be simple pits dug into the earth or nests or rocky caves.

13

Many dinosaurs had a small, functionless claw on their legs. It didn't touch the ground.

The longest dinosaurs were called sauropods. They were huge, slowmoving, tinyheaded, cowlike herbivores.

Sauropods had very long necks to reach the highest branches of the trees.

The tallest dinosaurs were
Brachiosaurid Sauropods.

Some dinosaurs were speedy like the Velociraptor. Some were slow like the Ankylosaurus.

Argentinosaurus, Ultrasauros, Brachiosaurus and Supersaurus were some of the largest and the tallest dinosaurs.

The smallest dinosaurs, like Compsognathus, were about the size of a chicken!

The oldest known dinosaur is Eoraptor.

The Troödons were probably the smartest dinosaurs.

Stegosaurus was the dumbest dinosaur. It had a brain the size of a walnut!

Utahraptor was the most violent of all the dinosaurs.

Some dinosaurs had plates all over their bodies. Even their eyelids had armour plating!

Many dinosaurs had deadly, knife-like spines on their bodies. These kept their enemies away.

Dinosaurs used their tails for balance.

Some dinosaurs used their tails to turn or change direction.

Some dinosaurs had bony knots
at the end of their tails. They
used their tails for defense.

No one knows for sure what colour the dinosaurs were as they lived many years before man.

Some dinosaur species lived in groups or herds.

New words to learn

reptiles

hatched

terrible

insectivore

omnivore

swallowed

prey

strong

sense

hunting

functionless

sauropods

Brachiosaurid

fibres

vegetation

Velociraptor

Ankylosaurus

Compsognathus

Eoraptor

smartest

enemies